W9-BNR-924

Monticello

by Michael Burgan

Thank you to the Monticello Education Department,
Thomas Jefferson Foundation,
Charlottesville, Virginia

Reading Adviser: Dr. Linda D. Labbo,
Department of Reading Education, College of Education,
The University of Georgia

COMPASS POINT BOOKS

Minneapolis, Minnesota

Compass Point Books
3109 West 50th Street, #115
Minneapolis, MN 55410

Visit Compass Point Books on the Internet at *www.compasspointbooks.com*
or e-mail your request to *custserv@compasspointbooks.com*

Photographs ©: Monticello/Thomas Jefferson Foundation, Inc., cover, 6, 10, 12, 29, 31; National
Portrait Gallery, Smithsonian Institution/Art Resource, N.Y., 4; William A. Bake/Corbis, 5; Buddy
Mays/Corbis, 8; Erich Lessing/Art Resource, N.Y., 11; Burstein Collection/Corbis, 13; North
Wind Picture Archives, 15; R. Lautman/Monticello, 16, 17, 19, 21, 24, 26, 27; Edward Owen/
Monticello, 18, 41; Lombard Antiquarian Maps & Prints, 20; Charles Shoffner/Monticello, 23;
Special Collections Department, University of Virginia Library, 32, 34; From Cincinnati's Colored
Citizens by Wendell P. Dabney, 1926, 33; Courtesy of Jim McMillan, 35; U.S. Naval Academy
Museum, 36; Library of Congress, 37; American Jewish Historical Society, Newton Centre,
Massachusetts, and New York, N.Y., 38; Holsinger Studio Collection, Special Collections
Department, University of Virginia Library, 39.

Editors: E. Russell Primm, Emily J. Dolbear, Halley Gatenby, and Catherine Neitge
Photo Researcher: Svetlana Zhurkina
Photo Selector: Linda S. Koutris
Designer/Page Production: Bradfordesign, Inc./Biner Design
Cartographer: XNR Productions, Inc.

Library of Congress Cataloging-in-Publication Data
Burgan, Michael.
   Monticello / by Michael Burgan.
     p. cm. — (We the people)
   Summary: Relates the history of Thomas Jefferson's home in central Virginia, including what
life was like there for himself, his family, their slaves, visitors, and descendants, and how
Monticello became a museum. Includes bibliographical references and index.
   ISBN 0-7565-0491-0 (alk. paper)
   1. Monticello (Va.)—History—Juvenile literature. 2. Jefferson, Thomas, 1743–1826—Homes
and haunts—Virginia—Albemarle County—Juvenile literature. [1. Monticello (Va.) 2. Jefferson,
Thomas, 1743–1826—Homes and haunts. 3. Jefferson family.] I. Title. II. Series: We the people
(Compass Point Books)
   E332.74.B87 2003
   975.5'482—dc21   2003001681

TABLE OF CONTENTS

NOTE: *In this book, words that are defined in the glossary are in* **bold** *the first time they appear in the text.*

A Special "Little Mountain"

The Blue Ridge Mountains cut through the western half of Virginia. On a hill near that mountain range sits one of the most famous homes in the United States. The hill, the house, and the land surrounding them are all known as Monticello (mon-teh-CHELL-oh). This Italian name means "little mountain."

Monticello was the beloved home of Thomas Jefferson, the third president of the United States. Jefferson was one of the greatest thinkers America has ever produced. He is most famous for his political writings,

Thomas Jefferson was the third president of the United States and the owner of Monticello.

4

A view of the Blue Ridge Mountains in Virginia

including the Declaration of Independence. Jefferson was also a scientist, an inventor, and an architect. At Monticello, he displayed all his talents.

Jefferson designed Monticello himself. He then spent many years adding on to it and changing it to fit his needs. Jefferson's duties in government often kept him away from

Monticello as it looks today

Monticello, but it remained special to him. From the house, looking west, he could see the mountains. Beneath the hill that Jefferson's house sat on, he saw the town of Charlottesville. He also marveled at the sight of the rising sun that he often viewed from his home.

All around Monticello were rich farmlands. Jefferson believed that farmers played an important role in American life. He said they were "the most independent, the most **virtuous** . . . they are tied to their country and wedded to its liberty." Jefferson proudly called himself a farmer, and his lands at Monticello produced a number of crops.

Monticello was a **plantation.** Hundreds of people worked and lived on Jefferson's property. The plantation buzzed with both manufacturing and farm activity. Most of the workers at Monticello were enslaved workers. Like many early U.S. leaders, Jefferson often talked of freedom, but he still accepted slavery. His enslaved workers played a key role inside and out of his home.

"HERE WAS BURIED
THOMAS JEFFERSON
AUTHOR OF THE
DECLARATION
OF
AMERICAN INDEPENDENCE
OF THE
STATUTE OF VIRGINIA
FOR
RELIGIOUS FREEDOM
AND FATHER OF THE
UNIVERSITY OF VIRGINIA"

BORN APRIL 2 743. O.S.
DIED JULY 4. 1826.

*Jefferson's grave is located on
the grounds of Monticello.*

8

In 1787, Jefferson wrote about Monticello, "I am as happy nowhere else and in no other society." He hoped to die at Monticello, and he got his wish in 1826. His body was buried on the home's grounds. Afterward, Jefferson's family could not afford to keep Monticello and sold it. At times, the house fell into **disrepair.** Today, however, Monticello looks as grand as it did when Jefferson lived there. Tourists explore the house and its gardens, and they can imagine the joy Monticello brought to its proud owner.

THE FIRST MONTICELLO

In 1764, when Jefferson was twenty-one years old, he inherited several thousand acres of land in Albemarle County, Virginia. This land included Shadwell, the farm where Jefferson was born, and the property at Monticello.

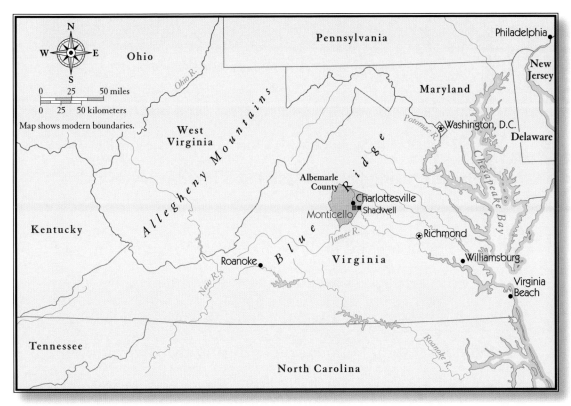

A map of Virginia and the surrounding area

9

A historical marker shows where Shadwell, which burned in 1770, once stood.

In 1768, he began clearing away trees on a hill he had admired since he was a child. On that spot, he built Monticello, using both enslaved and hired workers to make bricks and assemble the structure.

The house did not look like most Virginia homes of that time. Jefferson's **architecture** was influenced by Italian design. He especially liked the style of Andrea Palladio, who built several famous homes during the sixteenth century. Jefferson's work, like Palladio's, was similar in some ways to the architecture found in ancient Greece and Rome. Jefferson later called Monticello "an **essay** in architecture." He wanted the house to show his interests in classical architecture.

The San Giorgio Maggiore in Venice was designed by Italian architect Andrea Palladio.

11

Jefferson lived in South Pavilion while he waited for Monticello to be finished.

In 1770, the workers completed a small brick building called a pavilion. It was south of the main house. Jefferson lived in what he called the South Pavilion while work continued on the rest of the house. The original Monticello had fourteen rooms: five on the first floor, three on the second floor, and six in the cellar. Jefferson's study, or office, was on the second floor. The first floor featured the parlor, which was a living room where Jefferson entertained guests.

In 1772, Jefferson married Martha Wayles Skelton, and they soon began raising a family at Monticello. A few years later, Jefferson made the first major change to the home's design. He added on to the parlor and the second-story study above it. The new space was in the shape of an octagon, with three of its eight sides missing. (These sides were attached to the house). Jefferson then added a one-floor room with a similar shape to the ends of the house.

Work went on at Monticello during the Revolutionary War (1775–1783) when Jefferson was often away from home.

Colonists face British soldiers at the Battle of Bunker Hill during the Revolutionary War.

First, he traveled to Philadelphia, Pennsylvania, to serve as a member of the Continental Congress. While in Philadelphia, he was called upon to draft the Declaration of Independence. Jefferson later served as a legislator and as governor of Virginia, and lived in Williamsburg and Richmond. British troops invaded Virginia and took over Monticello for a short time in 1781. Jefferson and his family fled to the safety of Poplar Forest, a plantation inherited by Jefferson and his wife upon the death of her father.

By the time the war ended, most of the basic structure of Monticello was complete. Inside, workers continued to add details. A French visitor to the house said Monticello "resembled none of the others [houses] seen in this country." The guest added that Jefferson was "the first American who had consulted the Fine Arts to know how he should shelter himself from the weather."

In 1784, Jefferson left Monticello on a mission for the U.S. government and served as a **diplomat** in Europe.

Jefferson (center) at the signing of a treaty in France in 1778

For most of the next five years, Jefferson lived in France. When he returned to America, he served under President George Washington until 1793. Then he settled in at Monticello. Soon, though, the house would change again.

15

A NEW DESIGN

While in France, Jefferson was impressed with the homes he saw. Many had skylights to let sunlight stream in through the roof. Others had indoor **privies**— a rare sight in American homes at that time. Jefferson decided to add these features to Monticello. He also

Jefferson kept plants in Monticello's greenhouse.

wanted to expand the home. At the same time, however, Jefferson wanted it to look as if Monticello had only one story. This kind of design was also popular in France.

In 1796, workers began tearing down the second floor of Monticello. Then, within the existing first floor,

16

they added another floor. Here, Jefferson built several bed-rooms. He placed the beds in small spaces called **alcoves,** instead of in the center of the rooms. Other new rooms included a large entrance hall, a library, and a greenhouse.

On the new third floor, Jefferson built a dome-shaped room. Monticello was the first home in the United States to have a dome. The room had four round windows and a round skylight in the center of the ceiling. At different times, the dome room served as a bedroom, a playroom for children, and a storage area. The stairs leading to the room were narrow, and the room was sometimes left empty.

The unique dome room on the third floor was used for several different purposes.

17

John Hemings used his woodworking skills to make this chair.

The decorations at Monticello were completed during this time. James Dinsmore produced beautiful woodwork for the home. He had help from his assistant, John Hemings, who was a slave at Monticello. Hemings had started by working on the slave homes at Monticello. He learned the art of woodworking and later created much of the woodwork and furniture at Poplar Forest. Jefferson freed John Hemings in his will.

As Jefferson added on to Monticello, building went on outside the house, as well. Sometime after 1800, a **terrace** linked the South Pavilion to the main house and was named the South Terrace. Another terrace stretched from the house to the North Pavilion, which was completed in 1808. The terraces were long, wooden walkways. Shaped like an L,

they were built into
the side of the hill.
Jefferson built small
rooms underneath
them. These rooms
included a kitchen,
storage rooms, and
living areas for some
of Jefferson's slaves.

While the
major changes went
on, Jefferson spent

The kitchen of Monticello was located in the basement.

most of his time in Washington, D.C. In 1801, he was sworn
in as president of the United States. He held that office for
eight years. When he returned to Monticello in 1809, the
changes were done, and Jefferson was finally able to enjoy his
home. The expanded Monticello had forty-three rooms total:
thirty-three in the house itself, four in the pavilions, and six
under the South Terrace.

19

LIFE INSIDE MONTICELLO

Jefferson's wife, Martha, had died in 1782, but a number of relatives lived with him at Monticello. His daughter, Martha, her husband, Thomas Mann Randolph, and six of their eight children moved into the house when Jefferson settled there in 1809. The Randolphs later had three more children at Monticello. Jefferson's sisters, Anna and Martha, also spent time at the house.

Martha Randolph, Jefferson's daughter, lived at Monticello starting in 1809.

Jefferson wrote to John Adams, "I live in the midst of my grandchildren." His grandchildren must have enjoyed life at Monticello. John Hemings sometimes made toys and furniture for Jefferson's grandchildren. They ran races with their grandfather in the gardens. In the evenings, the family would sometimes sit in the parlor with guests. They would often play word games or board games, such as chess. Jefferson also loved music. He gave his granddaughter, Virginia, a guitar, and he sometimes played the violin while his grandchildren danced around him. On quieter nights, the family would simply read.

Jefferson had a steady stream of visitors. As many as fifty people sometimes stayed at Monticello, which had only twelve bedrooms! Two popular guests were James Madison and his wife, Dolley. Like Jefferson, Madison was a great political thinker,

This room was reserved for James Madison and his wife, Dolley, when they came to visit at Monticello.

and he served as the fourth U.S. president. The room where he stayed was known as "Mr. Madison's room." Another room was named for Abbé José Correia. He was a Portuguese scientist and diplomat who visited Monticello seven times. When Jefferson retired to Monticello after serving as president, the number of visitors increased. Sometimes he would escape to Poplar Forest to get some peace and quiet.

Guests entered Monticello through the Entrance Hall. This large room was like a minimuseum. Jefferson hung maps and European artwork on the walls. He showed off America's history with an engraving of the Declaration of Independence and John Trumbull's famous painting of the signing of the Declaration. There were bones of ancient North American animals. He also displayed Native American items such as carved figures, a painted buffalo robe, and a cradle. Many of these were sent from the West by explorers Meriwether Lewis and William Clark. The room in which they were displayed was sometimes called Jefferson's Indian Hall.

The Entrance Hall to Monticello contains artwork and historical items.

Jefferson, his family, and guests ate in either the Dining Room or the Tea Room. Most of the food served came from the Monticello plantation. Jefferson did not eat much meat. He preferred the vegetables and fruits from

23

Jefferson, his family, and guests ate some of their meals in the Dining Room.

his gardens. Jefferson also bought some items from over-
seas or at shops in Richmond. One treat in the Monticello
dining room was ice cream—a rare dessert in America at

24

that time. Most eighteenth-century American families had only two meals—breakfast and dinner. At Monticello, dinner was served in the late afternoon, followed by tea in the evening.

One guest said dinner was "in good taste and abundance." Although the women in Jefferson's family were in charge of deciding on a menu and overseeing the kitchen and household tasks, slaves did most of the work. One such slave was James Hemings, Jefferson's cook. He had accompanied Jefferson to France to train as a chef. Hemings then served as Jefferson's chef in France and Philadelphia, as well as at Monticello. When he asked Jefferson for his freedom, Jefferson had him train his brother, Peter Hemings, to take his place. James Hemings was one of two slaves Jefferson freed during his lifetime.

Jefferson liked to have his slaves out of sight while he ate. To help guests serve their food themselves, he used dumbwaiters. These were tables on wheels, with

A dumbwaiter was used to bring wine from the cellar to the dining room.

several shelves. Food was placed on the shelves, and guests then took the food as they were ready. A different kind of dumbwaiter was used to bring bottles of wine from the cellar to the first floor. The bottles went into a box attached to a rope. Pulling on the rope brought the box up to the Dining Room.

Guests were not allowed into one part of the house: the four rooms where Jefferson worked, studied, and slept. These included a private greenhouse and the Book Room, which was Jefferson's library. He once wrote, "I cannot live without books." By 1814, he owned more than six thousand of them. That year, the British attacked Washington,

D.C., during the War of 1812 (1812–1814). A fire destroyed the library at the U.S. Capitol, so Jefferson sold his books from Monticello to start a new library there. These books became part of the Library of Congress, which still exists today.

Jefferson's bed alcove opened onto two rooms. He could get out of bed into his bedroom or into his office.

THE MONTICELLO PLANTATION

While Jefferson and his guests dined or rested, activity went on all around them. The Monticello plantation was split into four separate farms. Jefferson first raised tobacco in his fields, as many Virginia planters did at that time. During the 1790s, he switched to wheat as his main crop. He studied the latest scientific methods of farming so the soil would remain healthy and produce good crops. He also raised sheep and hogs.

Jefferson was proud of the gardens of Monticello. He planned and cared for them with the help of a Scottish gardener, Robert Bailey, and Wormley Hughes, an enslaved gardener. There were flower gardens, a vegetable garden, fruit gardens, and vineyards. Not only did they provide Monticello with food and flowers, the gardens also served as Jefferson's laboratory. He could experiment with plants from all over the world, including Italy, France, and Mexico. Jefferson even received plants from the West that were sent to him by Lewis and Clark.

Trees were among Jefferson's favorite plants. When he lived in France, he gave out seeds of certain North American plants to his friends. At Monticello, Jefferson treated his guests to tours of the grounds—and to lectures on the many kinds of trees he had planted. One guest called them Jefferson's "pet trees." In addition to being beautiful, the trees at Monticello provided much-needed shade during the hot summers.

The huge vegetable garden provided food for Jefferson's family. Jefferson tried growing more than seventy types of

The vegetable garden at Monticello

vegetables. They included some common vegetables, such as carrots, tomatoes, beans, peas, and lettuce. Less common vegetables included kale and Jerusalem artichokes. The garden also produced herbs, and Jefferson grew a variety of fruit in his orchards. The plantation grounds included many flowers of different colors. One wildflower grown in the garden was named for Jefferson.

Jefferson encouraged his daughters and granddaughters to work in the flower gardens, accompanied by older slaves. At any time, about one hundred and twenty African-American slaves operated the Monticello plantation. Some also worked in the main house as servants and lived in rooms under the South Terrace.

Many of the slaves and white workers lived and worked in a series of small buildings on Mulberry Row. This area ran along the south side of the house. It was named for the mulberry trees growing nearby. The buildings included a dairy, a stable, a blacksmith shop, a **joinery,** and a carpentry shop. Some of the slaves at Monticello became skilled

This painting shows how Mulberry Row probably looked at the time Jefferson lived at Monticello.

carpenters, furniture makers, and blacksmiths. Jefferson also had his own textile, or cloth, shop. Workers there turned wool and cotton thread into cloth that was then used to make clothes for Monticello's slaves.

Jefferson had mixed feelings about slavery. He thought slavery should end—someday. However, he freed only a handful of the hundreds of slaves he owned during his life. Still, he believed he should "feed and clothe them well" and "require such reasonable labor only as is performed voluntarily by freemen."

Isaac Jefferson was an enslaved blacksmith at Monticello.

When the enslaved workers were not working for Jefferson, they grew their own crops, hunted, fished, made their own clothing and furniture, and raised chickens. At times, Jefferson bought some of their produce, eggs, and chickens for his own kitchen. The enslaved workers at Monticello labored six days a week but had Sundays and holidays free to do what they wanted. They spent these days playing games, practicing their religions, and singing and dancing. At Christmastime, they were sometimes allowed to visit other plantations or towns.

Some slaves learned how to read and write. Though teaching a slave to read was not a crime, it was not allowed by all slave owners at that time. Peter Fossett was a slave at

Monticello and was sold after Jefferson's death. He later remembered how his new master whipped any slaves caught reading. However, Fossett continued to learn and taught other slaves to read and write. After gaining his freedom, he became a **caterer** and used many of the recipes passed down from his mother, who had been a cook at Monticello.

Jefferson often owned entire families of slaves, with their children and grand-children working at Monticello. The most famous of these families was the Hemings family, which included James and Peter. Their sister, Sally, also worked inside the Jefferson home, and Jefferson may have fathered several children with her. In his will, Jefferson freed seven slaves. All of these were members of the Hemings family.

Peter Fossett was a slave at Monticello who eventually became a caterer once he gained his freedom.

33

DIFFICULT YEARS

Despite all the farming and other business activity at Monticello, Jefferson was often in debt. Over time, he let parts of Monticello become run down. A visitor in 1824 noted that the house was "rather old and going to decay." Outside, he said, "Appearances about his yard and hill are rather **slovenly.**"

Monticello fell into disrepair in the mid-1800s.

When Jefferson died in 1826, he owed different people about $100,000. To pay these debts, his grandson, Thomas Jefferson Randolph, sold Jefferson's slaves and most of the items inside Monticello. For several years, Monticello sat empty, waiting for a buyer. Finally, in 1831, a young man from Charlottesville named James Barclay bought Monticello for $7,000.

James Barclay bought Monticello in 1831.

Barclay tried to raise silkworms on the farm so he could produce silk thread for clothes. The business failed, however, and Barclay continued to let Monticello decay. During that time, and for years after, visitors and tourists stopped by the house to admire it and see where the great Thomas Jefferson had lived.

35

Commodore Uriah Levy admired Jefferson and bought Monticello in 1834.

In 1834, Barclay sold Monticello to Uriah Levy. A Jewish naval officer, Levy respected Jefferson because he believed Americans should be allowed to freely practice any—or no—religion. Levy did not want to live full time at Monticello. He saw it as his country home, where he would stay for vacations. Some of his relatives also stayed at Monticello.

Levy fixed up the house and hired people to work the farm. In 1838, a local newspaper noted that "with the exception of the terraces, the whole building is in good repair." Visitors continued to come to Monticello, and some were charged twenty-five cents to see the grounds. Over the years, Levy made sure his hired help kept the plantation looking good. However, Levy seemed to have bad luck in farming. In one letter, he complained, "The wheat has turned out badly, the tobacco crop will or has failed, the oats are all straw."

In 1861, Virginia and other Southern states broke apart from the Union to form their own country. This action led to the Civil War (1861–1865). Levy was not at Monticello when the war began. That October, the Confederate States of America—the government formed by the Southern states—took control of Monticello. At different times during the war, both Northern and Southern soldiers visited the house. Some took souvenirs or wrote their names on the walls. Once again, Monticello fell into disrepair.

A Civil War battle in Williamsburg, Virginia, in May 1862   **37**

A NEW LIFE

In 1862, Uriah Levy died. In his will, he left Monticello to the U.S. government. He wanted the country to use the house as a training school for the children of dead naval officers. Congress, however, did not want to take control of Monticello. At the same time, some of Levy's relatives were challenging his will in court. His brother, Jonas, led a legal battle that eventually gave Monticello to his son, Jefferson. He took complete control of Monticello in 1879. The local paper welcomed Jefferson Levy's plans "to put it in a thorough state of repair, keeping close as possible to the original plans and style."

Jefferson Levy took control of Monticello in 1879.

The dining room at Monticello at about the same time Jefferson Levy lived there

Levy was a wealthy businessman. He also served for six years in the U.S. House of Representatives. Like his uncle Uriah, Jefferson Levy deeply respected Thomas Jefferson. Several of the items Thomas Jefferson once owned at Monticello were sold after his death to pay debts. Levy bought some of these back and returned them to the home. Levy also bought land that had once been part of the plantation.

In 1900, some Americans suggested the government should buy Monticello and turn it into a national monument to honor Jefferson. In 1912, Congress began to actively pursue the idea. Levy, however, had no plans to sell it. He had spent large amounts of money to make it a beautiful home. His friends asserted that Levy had taken better care of the property than the government ever could.

In 1920, people once again tried to convince Levy to sell Monticello. By 1923, he was finally ready to sell. A group called the Thomas Jefferson Memorial Foundation paid $500,000 for the house so it could be opened to the public. The group collected donations to pay for the house and to keep it in good shape. In 1924, about twenty thousand people paid fifty cents apiece to visit Monticello.

Since then, the Thomas Jefferson Foundation has continued to own and take care of Monticello. During the 1950s, it added steel **joists** to support the floors and installed a new heating and cooling system. In general, though, the foundation has tried to keep the home and the grounds just as they were when Jefferson lived there.

The plantation is also a source of information about the past. **Archaeologists** working there have found where some slaves were buried. The scientists have also uncovered pits in the ground along what used to

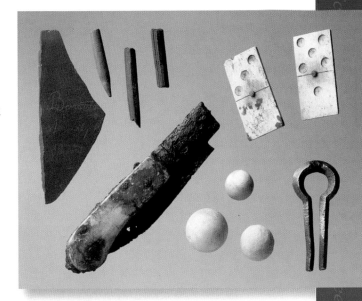

Items found by archaeologists in the pits along Mulberry Row

be Mulberry Row. The pits were storage areas used by the slaves who lived there. The archaeologists' discoveries help explain what slave life was like at Monticello.

Today, at least five hundred thousand people visit Monticello each year. They admire the beautiful scenery and learn about plantation life in the early nineteenth century. They see the unique home that belonged to a unique American. As one historian wrote, "No building in the world is more identifiable with a single mind."

41

GLOSSARY

alcoves—spaces built into walls

archaeologists—scientists who study people, places, and things of the past

architecture—the design of buildings

caterer—someone who owns or works for a service that prepares food

diplomat—a person who represents his or her government in a foreign country

disrepair—needing improvements or fixing

essay—a statement on a subject, usually written

joinery—where woodwork and furniture was shaped and joined

joists—supports under a floor or ceiling

plantation—a large farm in the South, usually worked by slaves

privies—toilets

slovenly—messy

terrace—an open porch or a paved area just outside a house

virtuous—having good, moral qualities

DID YOU KNOW?

- Friend and botanist William Bartram named one of the flowers at Monticello after Jefferson. The Jeffersonia, or twinleaf, grows to be about 12 inches (30 centimeters) tall.

- Thomas Jefferson tried to eat as little meat as possible. He included a wide variety of vegetables in his diet. Jefferson's granddaughter even said that he ate meat mainly to add flavor to his vegetables. When possible, he preferred dining upon what he grew in his own garden at Monticello.

- Jefferson wanted to paint the floor of the Entrance Hall of Monticello "grass-green." Another interesting feature of the entrance hall was the Great Clock, designed by Jefferson himself.

- By the early 1900s, Monticello was said to receive between forty thousand and fifty thousand visitors annually. Among these visitors was President Theodore Roosevelt, who came to Monticello in 1906.

IMPORTANT DATES

Timeline

1743	Thomas Jefferson is born at Shadwell in what is now Albemarle County, Virginia.
1764	Jefferson inherits several thousand acres of land in Albemarle County, Virginia.
1768	Jefferson begins clearing land to build Monticello.
1772	Jefferson marries Martha Wayles Skelton.
MID-1770s	Several rooms are added to Monticello.
1796	Work begins on a major addition to Monticello.
1800	The dome is constructed at Monticello.
1809	Jefferson retires to Monticello.
1826	Jefferson dies and is buried at Monticello.
1831	James Barclay buys Monticello from Jefferson's family.
1834	Uriah Levy buys Monticello and begins restoring it.
1879	Jefferson Levy becomes the new owner of Monticello.
1923	The Thomas Jefferson Memorial Foundation buys Monticello for $500,000.

IMPORTANT PEOPLE

JAMES BARCLAY
(1807–1874), *second owner of Monticello who tried to make a living raising silkworms on the property*

SALLY HEMINGS
(1773–1835), *slave at Monticello who may have had a relationship with Jefferson*

THOMAS JEFFERSON
(1743–1826), *third president of the United States (1801–1809) and the designer, builder, and original owner of Monticello*

JEFFERSON LEVY
(1852–1924), *Uriah Levy's nephew and the fourth and last private owner of Monticello*

URIAH LEVY
(1792–1862), *naval officer and Monticello's third owner who tried to leave the estate to the U.S. government*

MARTHA WAYLES SKELTON
(1748–1782), *Jefferson's wife*

WANT TO KNOW MORE?

At the Library

Heinrichs, Ann. *Thomas Jefferson.* Minneapolis: Compass Point Books, 2002.

Richards, Norman. *Monticello.* Chicago: Children's Press, 1995.

Stone, Lynn M. *Plantations.* Vero Beach, Fla.: Rourke Publications, 1993.

Young, Robert. *A Personal Tour of Monticello.* Minneapolis: Lerner Publications, 1999.

On the Web

For more information on *Monticello,* use FactHound

to track down Web sites related to this book.

1. Go to *www.facthound.com*

2. Type in a search word related to this book

    or this book ID: 0756504910.

3. Click on the *Fetch It* button.

Your trusty FactHound will fetch the best Web sites for you!

Through the Mail

The Corporation for Jefferson's Poplar Forest

P.O. Box 419

Forest, VA 24551

For information on the plantation itself, as well as details about the lives of Jefferson and the slaves who worked at Poplar Forest

On the Road

Monticello

Thomas Jefferson Parkway

P.O. Box 316

Charlottesville, VA 22902

publicaffairs@monticello.org

434/984-9822

To visit Jefferson's famous home, plantation, and gardens

INDEX

About the Author

Michael Burgan is a freelance writer of books for children and adults. A history graduate of the University of Connecticut, he has written more than sixty fiction and nonfiction children's books for various publishers. For adult audiences, he has written news articles, essays, and plays. Michael Burgan is a recipient of an Edpress Award and belongs to the Society of Children's Book Writers and Illustrators.